COCAINE

Sarah Lennard-Brown

Raintree

Chicago, Illinois

Copyright Permissions
Raintree
100 N. LaSalle
Suite 1200
Chicago, IL 60602

Design: Carole Binding
Photo research: Glass Onion Pictures
Printed in China. Bound in the United States.

09 08 07 06 05
1 2 3 4 5 6 7 8 9 0

Library of Congress Cataloging-in-Publication Data:

Lennard-Brown, Sarah.
  Cocaine / Sarah Lennard-Brown.
    p. cm. -- (Health issues)
  Includes bibliographical references and index.
   Contents: The story of cocaine use -- The
effects of cocaine -- Cocaine addiction --
Recovering from addiction -- Cocaine in today's
world.
  ISBN 0-7398-6893-4 (lib. bdg.)
  1. Cocaine--Juvenile literature. 2. Cocaine
habit--Juvenile literature. [1. Cocaine. 2. Drug
abuse.] I. Title. II. Series.
  HV5810.L45 2005
  362.29'8--dc22
                                2003026862

Acknowledgments
The author and publishers thank the following for their permission to reproduce photographs and illustrations: Cover and pp.1, 4 Corbis (Charles Gupton); pp.3, 19, 41, 46 Topham/ImageWorks (MR©John Griffin) p.5 Science Photo Library (Wesley Bocxe); p.7 Impact (Vera Lentz); p.10 Topham/Fotomas; p.12 Popperfoto; p.14 Corbis (Historical Picture Archive); p.16 Camera Press; p.18 Rex Features (Patrick Barth); p.20, 55 Rex Features (Sipa Press); p.22 Rex Features (Chat); p.24 Mediscan;p.28 Corbis (Nancy Ney); p.31 Rex Features (Raguet/Phanie); p.33 Corbis (Annie Griffiths Belt); p.36 Corbis (Ant Strack); p.37 Corbis (Tom Stewart); p.39 Corbis (Bill Gentile); p.43 Science Photo Library (Pascal Goetgheluck); p.45 Science Photo Library (Oscar Burriel); p.49 Impact (Simon Shepheard); p.50 Corbis (Steve Starr); p.52 Corbis (Tom Nebbia); p.57 Corbis (Tom and Dee Ann McCarthy); p.59 Angela Hampton Family Life Picture Library.
The illustrations on pages 27 and 32 are by Carole Binding.

Note: Photographs illustrating the case studies in this book were posed by models.

Every effort has been made to trace copyright holders. However, the publishers apologize for any unintentional omissions and would be pleased in such cases to add an acknowledgement in any future editions.

Contents

Introduction
What is Cocaine?

So much myth and fantasy has been woven around cocaine and its more recent derivatives, crack and freebase, that it can be difficult to separate fact from fiction. Cocaine was traditionally associated with the rich and famous. It was supposed to be the drug of choice for rock stars and celebrities. It was so expensive that using it was a sign of how wealthy you were. There are plenty of stories of parties with bowls of cocaine handed around and cocaine-fueled poolside celebrations.

The truth is not so glamorous. Cocaine, crack, and freebase are used by street gangs and the poorest members of society, as well as by the rich. They are all extremely addictive. Crack cocaine is reputedly the most addictive drug there is. People who become addicted to these drugs enter a world in which the only thing that matters is the next dose of drug, and they will do anything to get the money to buy more. Life is dangerous and often violent when they are "high," and it is fearful, sad, lonely, and miserable when they are not.

The high life

A popular image of cocaine has been that it is used mainly by the wealthy, including highly paid business-people.

Cocaine, crack, freebase, and drug mixes

Cocaine is usually produced as a crystalline white powder, though occasionally it is sold in the form of a paste. It is usually taken by sniffing the powder into the nose, known as "snorting."

Crack cocaine consists of large crystals, varying from white to a pinkish yellow.

Freebase is sold as a white powder and does not have as many impurities in it as crack or cocaine. Crack and freebase are usually smoked or heated and inhaled.

Drug mixes include one known as speedballs (a mixture of cocaine and heroin).

Cocaine, crack, and freebase are Schedule 1 Narcotics in the United States. This means that they are illegal drugs, and you can be prosecuted if you are found in possession of them.

The story of cocaine

Cocaine is made from a substance extracted from the leaves of coca plants, which grow in South America. From early times, people living in the Andes Mountains have chewed the leaves for the stimulating effects this gives. However, it was not until the 1850s that scientists purified the stimulant substance and created the drug called cocaine. There were high hopes for the new drug, particularly in the development of anesthetics. At the same time, people began to use the drug for its mind-changing effects. In chapter 1, you can find out more about the story of cocaine and the way attitudes toward its use have changed over time.

Market increase
Crack and freebase were developed by dealers eager to find more people who could afford their drugs.

Affecting the mind and body

Drugs that affect the brain, and therefore the mood and behavior of the user, are called psychoactive. Cocaine, crack, and freebase are psychoactive drugs that have a stimulant effect. This means that they make the user feel exhilarated, euphoric, and confident. People often become very talkative when they have taken cocaine and may feel very strong and energetic. However, they may also feel anxious and panicky. Cocaine can cause people to become violent and to have severe mental problems. Cocaine can also kill. Chapter 2 studies how cocaine, crack, and freebase affect the brain and the rest of the body in the experience of pleasure.

Addiction

Cocaine and its related drugs activate the parts of the brain that are activated by normal pleasures, and this is why the drugs are highly addictive. Users experience pleasure when they take the drug, followed by the absence of pleasure. This absence of pleasure is actually the result of having taken cocaine, but users do not realize this and take more cocaine to feel better again. They may become dependent on cocaine to feel any pleasure at all. In chapters 3 and 4, you can find out more about addiction to cocaine and how it can be treated.

Cocaine in today's world

In the final chapter we investigate the impact of cocaine, crack, and freebase on our world today. A very small proportion of the world's total population ever tries cocaine, and yet the drug has a profound impact on the lives and health of many people. For example, there are the people who live with addicts or in areas where crack users congregate. There are also those who live in cocaine-producing areas or who get caught up in drug-smuggling operations. On pages 58–59, we think about the real decisions that affect our lives today and evaluate the risks people take when they decide to try cocaine.

Street names

Cocaine
Coke, nose, blow, snow, snowflake, white lady, lady, Charlie, Candy, Big C, lines, Peruvian marching powder, Bolivian marching powder

Crack
Rocks, pebbles, scuds, flake, cloud nine, gravel, nuggets, Roxanne, bomb, coco puffs, dime pieces

Freebase
Base, baseball, freebase, beat, biscuit, bones, flame throwers

1 The Story of Cocaine Use
Past into Present

Cocaine is produced from the leaves of the South American coca bush *Erythroxylum coca.* The bush grows wild at high altitudes where there is substantial rainfall, such as in the Andes Mountains of Colombia, Bolivia, and Peru. It is grown legally and illegally in these countries, in blocks of two to three acres called "cocals." It is also grown illegally in mountainous areas of Southeast Asia and India.

Chewing coca leaves

Coca bush leaves have been chewed by the people of South America for about 5,000 years. They discovered that the stimulating effect of chewing the leaves could help them survive unpleasant physical sensations they experienced when climbing high into the mountains. Coca leaves contain a very low level of the active substance that makes cocaine so powerful. Each leaf contains approximately 2 percent of the substance, locked within the cell structure of the plant. To release the substance, the Andes people

Harvesting
In Peru, it is legal to harvest coca leaves for chewing and to make coca tea.

developed a special method of chewing the coca leaf. First, they burned seashells to make a chemical called lime. They ground it to a powder and kept it in a gourd hung around their waists. The gourd was sealed with a stick that dipped into the lime. Coca users would lick the stick, dip it into the lime, and spread a small layer of lime onto a leaf. The lime broke down the plant's cell structure releasing the substance. The leaf was then folded and chewed slowly for about 45 minutes. Afterward, the waste was spat out.

Chewing coca leaves was seen in the same way as drinking coffee or tea is today. Coca was chewed after a meal and between meals. The use of coca leaves was so much a part of life in the Andes that, for many tribes, getting your own gourd and coca pouch was a sign of maturity.

In the 16th century, Spanish invaders reached South America, and much of the continent became part of the

Cocaine Timeline

c. 3000 B.C.E.	Coca chewing becomes popular among the people of the Andes.
1400s C.E.	The Inca people of Peru farm coca.
Early 1500s	Inca coca plantations are taken over by Spanish invaders. The Spanish authorities tax coca production. Reports of the properties of the coca leaf reach Europe.
c. 1575	Laborers in South American silver mines are given coca leaves as payment.
1708	Coca is included in a dictionary of medicinal plants by German Herman Boerhaave.
1855	Cocaine is extracted from coca leaves by German scientist Friedrich Gaedcke.
1859	The extraction process is improved by Albert Niemann.
1862	E. Merck Company produces a quarter-pound of refined cocaine.
1869	Seeds of the coca plant become part of the botanical collection at Kew Gardens, London.
1880	Russian doctor Vasili von Anrep discovers the anesthetizing properties of cocaine.

Spanish Empire. At first, the Spanish tried to outlaw the use of coca. Christian priests felt that it was sinful and that it encouraged immoral behavior and laziness. Eventually, though, Spanish officials saw an opportunity to make money and took over the production of coca leaf. It was used as a form of currency—for example, to pay workers in the silver and gold mines. It is still common practice and lawful for people in the Andes to chew coca leaf, but cocaine production and use are illegal, as they are in the rest of the world.

Chewing coca leaves did not catch on in Europe. The leaves did not travel well. They became stale and unusable after the long sea journey to Spain. Also, chewing and spitting were (and still are) considered bad manners in the United States and most European countries.

Legal use

The Peruvian government authorizes farmers to cultivate small amounts of coca leaves for the purposes of chewing the leaves and making coca-leaf tea.

1884	Cocaine is first used as a local anesthetic in eye surgery. The psychiatrist Sigmund Freud publishes his ideas about cocaine in a book called *On Coca*.
1886	Coca-Cola®, containing cocaine syrup and caffeine, is launched onto the market.
1901	Cocaine is removed from the Coca-Cola® recipe.
1905	It becomes fashionable to snort cocaine.
1909	Cocaine is used on the Antarctic expedition of Sir Ernest Shackleton.
1910	Medical journals first report cases of nasal damage due to snorting cocaine.
1911	U.S. government reports 5,000 cocaine-related deaths.
1924	Second International Opium Conference at The Hague includes cocaine in a list of drugs that should have their production and use reduced.
1976	Freebase cocaine is developed.
1980s	Crack cocaine is developed. Crack and freebase become popular.
2002	The U.S. Department of Health and Human Services reports that the numbers of adolescents using illicit drugs declined from 15 percent in 1997 to 9.7 percent in 2000.

The creation of cocaine

Cocaine itself was not produced until 1855, when the German scientist Friedrich Gaedcke figured out how to extract and purify the active substance from the coca leaf. Another German, Albert Niemann, improved the process in 1859. Both scientists were interested in the medical properties of the drug, particularly its ability to relieve pain. At this time there were no real anesthetics to prevent patients from feeling pain during surgery. Surgery had to be carried out very fast, or the patient could die as a result of the pain. The need to work so fast made it impossible for surgeons to be very careful and accurate. Therefore, the search for an anesthetic that would allow less painful, more accurate surgery was very important. In 1880 a Russian doctor, Vasili von Anrep, discovered the anesthetizing properties of cocaine, and the Western world became increasingly interested in the drug.

Sigmund Freud recommends cocaine

One of the most famous people to become fascinated with the new drug was the psychiatrist Sigmund Freud. In 1884 he published *On Coca,* the first study of the effects of cocaine. While living in Vienna (Austria), he experimented with taking the drug himself and recorded what happened. At first he was very enthusiastic. The

Dental agony
Before the introduction of anesthetics, doctors and dentists could do little to lessen the pain of surgery. Alcohol was generally used to dull the patient's senses.

drug gave him lots of energy and made him feel euphoric, and he felt that it might help his friend, Ernst von Fleischl-Marxow, overcome his addiction to the drug morphine. This was a disaster. Ernst quickly became heavily addicted to cocaine. He took more and more, becoming the first person on record to develop a mental illness called cocaine-induced psychosis. In this illness, the sufferer experiences disturbing and frightening thoughts that seem so real to them that they may behave in strange and frightening ways. After this, Freud's opinion of cocaine changed, and he regarded it as potentially dangerous.

Freud helped the development of ophthalmic (eye) surgery when he reported the anesthetic qualities of cocaine to his friend, ophthalmologist (eye specialist) Carl Koller. Cocaine paste (a more dilute form of cocaine) was found to be very useful as a local anesthetic in eye surgery. It is still used as a local anesthetic in some eye, ear, nose, and dental operations today. It is sometimes mixed with other drugs and applied directly to the area requiring anesthetic.

Sigmund Freud

Sigmund Freud (1856–1939) studied medicine at the University of Vienna. He specialized in psychiatry. Some of his 1890s case studies about hysteria are thought to be the first examples of psychoanalysis. This is when a psychiatrist and a patient try to find the root of a patient's problem by talking. Freud felt that many psychiatric problems were caused by childhood trauma and unconscious urges and needs. Between 1896 and 1901, Freud worked on the details of his theory of psychoanalysis and developed more new ideas about how our minds work. It was Freud who came up with the idea of the unconscious and conscious mind and who first examined how our experiences affect the way we think and act. Many of Freud's ideas have since been proven wrong, but he is still considered the father of modern psychoanalysis and an influential thinker.

Popular use of cocaine

About 1880 many new products containing small amounts of processed cocaine became available across the United States and Europe. These included syrups and wines, tonics, and lozenges for treating coughs and sore throats. In 1886 a new drink, Coca-Cola®, was created. It was made from a secret recipe including cocaine-laced syrup and caffeine. It rapidly became a very popular soft drink, and it continued to contain cocaine syrup until it was removed from the formula in 1901.

Cocaine became famous for its stimulating properties. Cocaine pills called "Forced March" were used by members of the Antarctic expedition led by Sir Ernest Shackleton in 1909. The pills were supposed to help the explorers keep going under difficult conditions. Cocaine products were also used to improve the endurance of athletes, especially runners. In the early 20th century, cocaine was used by athletes in preparation for matches as well as in training. This was before people became aware of the dangers of cocaine or of issues about drug use in sports.

Changing ideas about drug use

In the late 19th century, experimenting with drugs was not considered shocking and was not illegal. However, taking drugs was disapproved of and thought to be a sign of "moral depravity" or a "weak mind." In 1887 the British writer Sir Arthur Conan Doyle published the first of many stories about the fictional detective Sherlock Holmes. In the stories, Holmes is addicted to cocaine, and the narrator, Dr. Watson, warns him of the (then) little-known dangers of long-term cocaine use. Holmes eventually manages to stop using cocaine in the stories in 1896. Conan Doyle is

Antarctic survival

Sir Ernest Shackleton (1874–1922) made four expeditions to the Antarctic. In 1909, when he almost reached the South Pole, he and his team of explorers took pills containing cocaine to help them endure the polar conditions.

sometimes criticized for portraying a hero as a drug user. However, others feel that he was showing the spirit of self-experimentation that was common at the time.

Snorting (sniffing cocaine into the nose) became popular about 1905, when patents on the process of producing cocaine, taken out by the company E. Merck, expired. This meant that anyone could now make cocaine, using Merck's process. Cocaine became cheaper and started to be used by the young and wealthy in the United States and Europe. In 1910 British medical journals included the first reports of nasal damage due to snorting, and, in 1912, the U.S. government recorded more than 5,000 deaths due to cocaine use in one year.

During the late 19th and early 20th centuries, the world was waking up to the health and social problems caused by drug addiction. Addiction to opium had already caused enormous problems in China and Egypt. Now the availability of narcotic drugs was seen to be causing a growing rate of addiction and many deaths in the United States and Europe. Representatives of many countries discussed how to tackle the international drug problem. At the Second International Opium Conference in 1924, they agreed to make laws to try to reduce the use of narcotic drugs. Over the following decades, many countries outlawed the production, sale, and possession of drugs, including heroin, cocaine, opium, and marijuana. However, there were still people prepared to break the law and risk prison because they saw a chance to make a large profit, selling the drugs to people who were addicted or could be persuaded to try them. It is illegal to grow coca leaves in nearly all countries, except some in South America, such as Peru and Bolivia, where small-scale growing of coca is allowed on cultural and religious grounds.

In and out of fashion

Because it was expensive to import and refine, cocaine was (and still is) an expensive drug. Only rich people could afford to buy it, and so taking cocaine became a sign that someone

Cocaine in popular culture

References to cocaine in popular music and culture are evidence that it has been a fashionable drug. First, the drug was featured in the Sherlock Holmes stories by Sir Arthur Conan Doyle in the late 19th century. In the 1930s a song by Cole Porter, "I Get a Kick Out of You," referred to cocaine. The drug came into fashion again in the 1960s, with the psychedelic movement, and in the 1970s, at which time Eric Clapton released the song "Cocaine."

Elementary

For the first ten years of writing his Sherlock Holmes stories, Sir Arthur Conan Doyle presented the fictional detective as a cocaine user.

was wealthy. In the 1920s, after World War I, society in the United States and Europe was sharply divided between the rich and poor. As the poor struggled to make a living, the rich (or, more often, the children of the rich) tried to forget the horror and grief of the war and had the time, money, and contacts to buy cocaine. However, the dangers of cocaine soon became obvious. Because it was wealthy and famous people who died from cocaine overdose, their stories appeared in the newspapers. People therefore became aware of the problems associated with cocaine, and it fell out of fashion. By the 1940s a police officer working as a narcotics supervisor in New York reported that he rarely heard of cocaine being used. In the 1950s the situation changed again. The world was recovering from World War II. Young people had more money to spend than ever before and were determined to forget the experience of wartime. Once more, cocaine use shot up, and then it rapidly decreased once the dangers and addictions became obvious.

The development of crack and freebase

In the 1970s and 1980s new forms of cocaine, called crack and freebase, were developed by dealers looking for more people to whom they could sell drugs. Crack and freebase were easily made from cocaine, and the method produced a greater amount of drug—although this was largely made up of baking soda, which was used in the process. The new forms of cocaine could be smoked. The effects were felt more quickly, but lasted for a shorter time, than when cocaine was snorted. Cocaine and crack became popular among drug addicts in Hollywood and were fashionable again. Because crack and freebase were cheaper to produce, they were seen as "downmarket." They became popular among gangs in inner-city areas of the United States. Cocaine became briefly popular among wealthy city businesspeople in the United States and Europe and celebrities who could afford it. Then, the risk of addiction and other dangers were publicized in the media, and the drug again went out of fashion.

"Smoking crack—it's hard to describe. You go from heaven to hell in the space of fifteen minutes. It changes your head, it's a road to disaster. Don't do it."
(Sonny, recovering crack addict)

Where does cocaine come from today?

The United Nations estimates that the world's cultivation of coca leaves went down by 17 percent in the 1990s. Most cocaine production takes place in the South American

The price of cocaine

Since cocaine was first produced in 1862, its price has varied enormously. Sometimes it is very expensive, due to the difficulty growing, processing, and smuggling it and the high profits demanded by "drug bosses." Between 1990 and 2000 the street price of a gram of cocaine varied between approximately $70 and $175. Since 1990 the prices of cocaine, crack, and freebase have come down. Crack cocaine is sold in "rocks"—large crystals that can be subdivided into "boulders" and "pebbles." A rock of crack sold for between $5 and $20 in the 1990s.

countries of Peru, Colombia, and Bolivia, with smaller areas of production in Brazil, Guyana, and Venezuela. There was a 40 percent reduction of cocaine production in Peru in the 1990s. Bolivia has reduced the area of land producing coca leaf by 50 percent. However, coca leaf production in Colombia has increased.

Colombia is now responsible for two-thirds of the world's coca leaf production and about 80 percent of cocaine manufacturing. Gangs of people who produce, smuggle, and supply cocaine are known as drug cartels and are usually led by powerful drug bosses, or "drug lords." The cartels are wealthy and pay for mercenaries (hired soldiers) to protect the areas where they grow cocaine. This leads to violence and conflict, and the people in these areas live in fear and uncertainty. The majority of the cocaine produced in South America is smuggled into the United States, while smaller amounts go to Europe and Australia. Of the total amount of cocaine seized by the police in 1997–1998, 83 percent was seized in the United States and 11 percent in Europe.

"There is often fighting around my town. People are killed and their homes are burned. The rebels grow coca in the mountains and are trying to take control of this area away from the government." (Gabrielle, age 10, Colombian student)

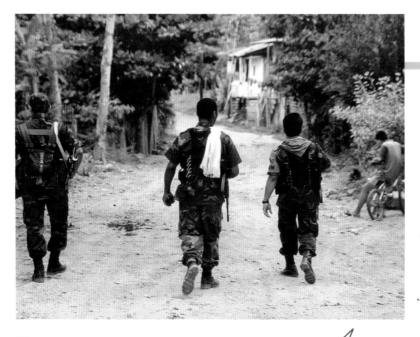

Daily life in Colombia

Rebel soldiers patrol a town in Colombia. Fighting between rebels (funded by cocaine smuggling) and the government in Colombia has been going on for more than 40 years. Over 30,000 people have been killed in the fighting.

Who uses cocaine?

A lot fewer people use cocaine than you might expect based on its high profile in the media. The United Nations Office on Drugs and Crime estimates that 180 million people worldwide over the age of fifteen consumed drugs at some point during the late 1990s. This is about 4.2 percent of the world's population. The most commonly used drug was marijuana (144 million users), followed by amphetamine-type stimulants (29 million users). By contrast, cocaine had only 14 million users worldwide (approximately 0.3 percent of the world's population).

During the late 20th century, cocaine use around the world was stable or decreasing, except in a few areas. It is thought that cocaine consumption fell by 70 percent in the United States between 1985 and 1999. The only places where cocaine use increased were certain areas in "transit countries" such as Mexico, other central and southern American countries, parts of southern and western Africa, and Eastern Europe. Transit countries are the countries used by the drug cartels to smuggle cocaine into the United States, Western Europe, and Australia. Since the end of the 20th century, cocaine use in the United Kingdom seems to have risen; customs officers seized more cocaine than heroin, and 6 percent of people between the ages of 16 and 29 tried the drug, compared to the 1 percent who tried heroin or crack cocaine (according to the British Crime Survey, 1999).

Figuring out who takes cocaine in the general population is difficult. Most cocaine users are occasional users and do not come to the attention of the authorities or health services. Therefore, they do not appear in official drug-use statistics. Cocaine remains fairly expensive, and so its users tend to be

Drug use around the world

Drug	% of world population (Over the age of 15) using the drug during 1990s
All illegal drugs	4.2%
Marijuana	3.3%
Amphetamines	0.7%
Cocaine	0.3%

(The United Nations Office on Drugs and Crime World Drug Report 2000)

wealthy. If they need treatment for their cocaine habit, they tend to pay for it privately and, again, they are not recorded in the statistics. There is no quick medical cure for cocaine addiction, and so there is little incentive for addicts to approach drug agencies for help. Regular surveys by the United Kingdom–based organization DrugScope have found that there is little use of cocaine among schoolchildren or older adults, but that up to a quarter of people attending nightclubs have tried cocaine.

It seems that the majority of cocaine users across the world are white males between the ages of 16 and 24, living in urban areas. The number of women reporting ever having tried cocaine is approximately half the number of men. Use of cocaine by groups younger than 16 and older than 35 is very small.

Dance scene cocaine use

"It always used to be ecstasy that people offered you at clubs. Some of my friends used to do it, but I never liked it. I didn't like the risk—we'd all heard about people who died after taking one ecstasy tablet, and so I never took any. But now it's changing. I guess because no one took ecstasy anymore, they tried something new. I didn't realize coke was dangerous. The guy who sold it said it couldn't harm you. I'd just feel great. Well, I did feel great at first, and it stopped me from eating. But later I'd feel terrible—there was nothing worse. A friend of mine told me about what she'd learned at school, about it being addictive like heroin and stuff. So I stopped. It's no good taking things that mess with your head. And you can never believe those dealers—they'd say anything if it made you buy some."
(Leanne)

2 The Effects of Cocaine
Risks to Body and Mind

How do people take cocaine?

Cocaine is usually sold in the form of a white powder. The user takes it by snorting, which means sniffing the powder into the nose. It is absorbed by the mucous membranes lining the nose, and from there it enters the bloodstream and travels to the brain. Another method some people use to take the cocaine powder is to rub it onto their gums or other mucous membranes.

Some people inject cocaine into their body. This involves dissolving the drug in a liquid and injecting it either into a vein or into the fat layer just below the skin. When the drug is injected into a vein, it gets into the bloodstream immediately, and so its effects are felt much faster than with other methods. As with injecting any drug, there are risks of infection with viruses such as hepatitis and HIV if needles are not sterile. Injecting can also damage veins and arteries. To make cocaine dissolve in a fluid, so that it can be injected, the mixture has to be heated. However, cocaine is easily broken down by heat. For this reason, injecting cocaine is not a popular method of taking the drug, since it is easy to destroy the cocaine and waste a lot of money in the process. Coca paste is rare, but it is usually smoked in a pipe called a bong. Again,

Preparing cocaine

Taking cocaine is often made into a ritual, using the same procedure every time. Some users always use the same equipment, such as a particular mirror or plate. Some always use a credit card, or a razor blade, to arrange the lines of drug for snorting. Some people snort cocaine from a specially shaped spoon.

Dangers of injecting cocaine

Apart from the danger of overdosing, the biggest risk of injecting cocaine comes from sharing needles and syringes with other drug users. Body fluids on and in shared equipment can pass infections such as HIV and hepatitis B and C from one person to another. Other dangers include infections at the injection site, septicemia (a life-threatening infection of the blood), endocarditis (an infection of the heart), and gangrene (a tissue-destroying bacterial infection). Injecting can also damage tissue around the injection site, especially if the same areas are used repeatedly, and eventually the tissue may die (necrosis). Repeated tissue damage from injections can also lead to blood clots in the veins (thrombosis) and inflammation of veins (phlebitis).

In many countries there are needle-exchange programs that aim to reduce the spread of diseases such as HIV and hepatitis. They allow injecting drug users to exchange their dirty needles for sterile ones and encourage them to use the new needle only once.

because cocaine breaks down when it is heated, the effects of the drug are reduced by this method.

How do people take crack and freebase?

Crack and freebase are able to withstand the temperatures reached during smoking. However, if the smoking temperature becomes too high, even these forms of cocaine will break down, and the drug will not produce the desired effect. Therefore, crack and freebase smokers have developed several methods to try to keep the temperature as low as possible. Some use bongs, which are also commonly used by marijuana smokers. These pipes have a water-filled chamber through which the vapor is drawn before it is inhaled. Another method of taking crack and freebase is to place the drug in a glass tube or on glass or metal foil and warm it with a match or lighter. This produces a vapor, which the user then inhales.

Vapors

Crack or freebase are sometimes warmed in a glass tube or pipe with vapors and then inhaled.

Immediate effects

Cocaine is a stimulant drug, and that is exactly what it does to the body. It stimulates it, speeding everything up. People who have taken cocaine become very active and talkative. They feel energetic and have a sense of euphoria (an extreme sense of well-being), which can be very pleasurable. Users often claim that they can see things remarkably clearly when they have taken the drug. This feeling, which is just another effect of the drug, can mislead people into making unsafe decisions—for example, to participate in casual sex or dangerous stunts. Cocaine stimulates all the systems of the body, including the heart rate and blood pressure, and this can be very dangerous to the user.

Effects of taking cocaine

Short-term effects	Long-term effects	Overdose
Energy	Heart disease	Irregular heartbeat
Euphoria	Stroke	Convulsions
Talkativeness	Damage to the nasal septum,	Heart failure
Heightened awareness	the strip of tissue that	Respiratory arrest
of surroundings	divides the nose into	(breathing stops)
Feelings of strength	nostrils	Coma
Fast heartbeat	Depression	Death
High blood pressure	Anxiety	
Facial numbness	Cocaine psychosis (strange	
Tremors (shaking)	and frightening thoughts	
Headache	that can result in strange	
Faster breathing	and violent behavior)	
Anxiety	Paranoia	
Irritability	Hallucinations	
Paranoia	Repetitive movements	
Depression	(repetitive picking or	
Weakness	stroking of body parts)	
Increased chance of stroke	Infertility	
and heart attack	Malnutrition	
	Infections	

Although the effects of cocaine are felt almost immediately, they can take 30 minutes to develop fully after snorting. The drug is broken down by the body very fast, so, within an hour, about half of the dose has broken down and is no longer capable of affecting the brain. Cocaine mimics the effects of the body's sympathetic nervous system. This is sometimes called the "fight-or-flight" response, because it primes your body to stand and fight or run away from danger. It speeds up your heart and makes sure your muscles have lots of energy (glucose) so that you can run fast. It also makes your lungs breathe more quickly and efficiently, to supply extra oxygen to the muscles so that they can operate effectively. Cocaine causes massive activation of the fight-or-flight response, to the extent that it can cause an irregular heartbeat, a heart attack, or a stroke (when a blood clot causes the death of some brain tissue). All of these can be fatal.

Crash landing

When the first effects of cocaine wear off, the user is left feeling weak, anxious, and depressed.

The enormous high produced by cocaine is followed by an equally enormous low, as the drug passes through the user's system. Users are left feeling weak, anxious, and depressed. This "crash" often makes them want to take more of the drug in order to feel good again, and so a cycle of using starts. The high-low cycle can lead users to keep on taking the drug until they have none left or until their system becomes so poisoned by the drug that they die.

The dangers of snorting

When cocaine is snorted, users may notice that, at first, their faces become numb, a feeling that passes after a few minutes. This is because of the anesthetizing properties of cocaine. Over time, snorting cocaine damages the nose. The drug causes the blood vessels in the nose to narrow. Blood supply is therefore reduced, and ulcers can develop inside the nose. As the ulcers spread, long-term cocaine snorting leads to the gradual destruction of the nasal septum, the strip of cartilage

"You can never tell exactly what a 'hit' will be like. It depends how strong the cocaine is and what it's been cut with. Sometimes I don't think there's any coke in it at all. Other times it's so strong, it's scary."
(Eva, regular cocaine user)

The risks of adulterated drugs

Cocaine powder is rarely 100 percent pure—in other words, not all the powder is actually cocaine. Dealers have usually diluted it, to varying degrees, with a "filler" substance, something that is a white powder like cocaine but not as expensive. This puts users at risk in several ways. First, they can never be sure how strong the drug is. If they take cocaine that has not been diluted as much as they are used to, it is possible that they will overdose.

Another risk is from the substances used as filler. Sometimes this is white flour or talcum powder or other cheaper drugs such as amphetamines. None of these substances is harmless. Snorting flour or talc into your lungs can cause lung disease. Some substances used as filler can cause severe injury or kill you.

that separates the nostrils. Some heavy cocaine users are left with a very large hole in the nasal septum, which may need surgical repair.

Cocaine and heart disease

Heart disease can result from long-term cocaine use, since the drug speeds up the development of fatty deposits (atherosclerosis) inside blood vessels. As the

Blood vessels

The narrowing of blood vessels is called vasoconstriction. Taking cocaine causes vasoconstriction in the nose, in the lining of the stomach, and even in the intestines, leading to ulcers and internal bleeding.

Nasal damage
A damaged nasal septum affects people's breathing. It also alters the way they sound when speaking or singing.

fatty deposits increase, the heart has to work harder to pump the blood through narrower tubes. This can cause the heart to grow larger (the heart muscle gets bigger as it has to work harder) and weaker, resulting in heart failure. Also, as the fatty deposits become larger, they can either block a blood vessel entirely, or they can break off and travel through the blood system until they get lodged in a narrow blood vessel. This can cause a stroke (a blockage in the blood vessels of the brain) or a heart attack. Deep vein thrombosis (a blockage of the veins in the leg) or pulmonary embolism (a blockage of the blood supply to the lungs) can be caused by complications following injecting cocaine into a vein. All of these can be fatal or can leave the person with a permanent disability.

The effect of cocaine on mental health

Cocaine can affect the mental health of users. Long-term cocaine users tend to have an increased level of paranoia (feeling that people are out to get them) and can suffer from severe depression. Some long-term users experience a condition called cocaine psychosis, when they lose contact with reality, are haunted by fear, and have hallucinations. These hallucinations often involve the idea that there are insects trapped under their skin. In order to get rid of these unreal creatures, people may scratch at their skin, giving themselves large wounds. People with cocaine psychosis are often aggressive and violent and may require hospital treatment to prevent them from harming themselves or others.

Some other long-term effects of cocaine use

There are some problems associated with using cocaine that are not directly caused by the drug. Cocaine tends to reduce appetite and increase activity, and so long-term

Like a wild animal

"The night Andy flipped out was one of the scariest of my life. We'd been out partying and having a good time. I knew Andy did coke occasionally, but I don't like drugs, so he didn't tell me he'd scored (bought some) and snorted it in the bathroom. He was okay for awhile, a little hyper, dancing like crazy—but Andy's like that. Then everything went crazy. He said that his drinks were poisoned, and that we had to protect him. He was really scared and jumpy. We tried to get him home, but then he turned on us, saying we were going to kill him. One of my friends held his arm and he hit out like a wild animal. We couldn't hold him and he ran off. The police picked him up eventually. It was terrible—I didn't know drugs could do that to you." (Steve)

users are often tired and undernourished. As a result, their resistance to infectious diseases is reduced. They tend to become ill more often and take longer to recover.

Patterns of behavior caused by using cocaine have a health cost, too. Cocaine use can increase the desire for sexual intercourse. This may result in the user having unprotected sex with many different partners. Some people may become involved in prostitution in order to get money to pay for cocaine. This puts people at high risk of developing sexually transmitted diseases, including HIV.

The action of cocaine in the brain

Cocaine use has a profound effect on the way the brain works. The effects of cocaine, including feeling good (euphoria), fast heartbeat, decreased appetite, and increased ability to concentrate, all occur because the drug stimulates the production of a group of chemicals in the brain called monoamine neurotransmitters. These chemicals are involved in transmitting signals between different nerves in the brain. Nerves are the structures in your body that communicate between your body and brain, and this is one of the ways in which your brain can control what your body is doing. For example, if you want to pick up a pencil, your brain sends messages through your network of nerves to tell the muscles of your arm and fingers what to do. There are many nerves around your body, and they all pass information to your brain. Neurotransmitters are the chemicals in your brain that pass the message on from one nerve in the brain to the next.

The neurotransmitters affected by cocaine include serotonin, noradrenalin, and dopamine. Cocaine increases the amount of these neurotransmitters at the nerve junctions, called synapses, and this excites the nerve endings so that they send out more signals. The result is that the person feels excitable, jumpy, and full of energy. Each neurotransmitter affects different behaviors.

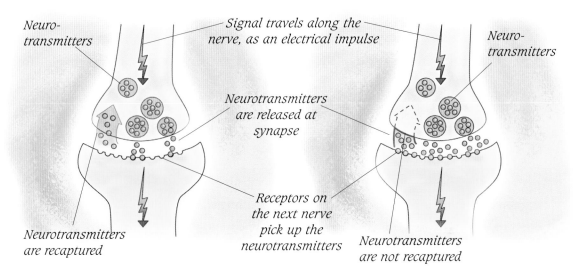

Normal function of nerves in the brain

Neuro-transmitters

Signal travels along the nerve, as an electrical impulse

Neurotransmitters are released at synapse

Receptors on the next nerve pick up the neurotransmitters

Neurotransmitters are recaptured

How cocaine affects this functioning

Neuro-transmitters

Neurotransmitters are not recaptured

⚫ *The effects of serotonin*

Serotonin helps your body get ready for sleep and plays a big part in regulating your body clock. Your body clock is an important mechanism that keeps your body functioning in rhythm. It controls your body temperature, lowering it at night and raising it in the morning to ensure you have the energy to get out of bed and face the day. It also controls your sleep cycles, helping to make you feel tired in the evening and get the right amount of deep sleep and dream sleep so that you feel refreshed in the morning. Your body clock is also involved in appetite regulation. It makes you feel hungry at certain times when your body is used to being fed, such as at breakfast, lunch, and dinner.

Cocaine disrupts the production of serotonin, and this upsets the body clock, first making users feel wide awake at night and taking away their appetite, and afterward leaving them extremely sleepy and hungry.

Cocaine and the neurotransmitters

This is a simplified drawing of how signals are passed from one nerve in the brain to the next, normally (left) and when the person has taken cocaine (right). Cocaine greatly increases the amount of neurotransmitters that are released at the synapses (junctions between nerves). It also stops the normal process through which neurotransmitters are recaptured.

● *The effects of noradrenalin (norepinephrine)*

Noradrenalin is one of several hormones produced when you have a shock. It is related to the hormone epinephrine, which makes your heart beat faster and your skin turn pale and clammy. (Epinephrine production is also triggered by cocaine, but this takes place in your adrenal glands, not in your brain.) Noradrenalin is involved in controlling the way you behave in an emergency. It regulates the amount of energy available to your muscles and brain. It widens the passages in your lungs to help you get more oxygen into your body. It also helps you to feel full of energy and enthusiasm, and to pay more attention to the world around you to help you get yourself out of danger. Noradrenalin reduces your appetite because, if you are in danger, it is not helpful to be distracted by hunger.

Cocaine increases the amount of noradrenalin available in the brain, and this again stops users from feeling hungry, speeds up their heart rate, and gives what is often described as a "rush" of excitement.

Happy feelings

Laughing and happy social interaction produce dopamine, the pleasure-giving brain chemical.

⬤ *The effects of dopamine*

Dopamine is the chemical messenger produced in your brain when you feel happy. If there is not enough dopamine, you feel sad. Dopamine is very important in what doctors call the brain's "reward system." According to this idea, dopamine is produced when you do something pleasurable—for example, eating, laughing, or dancing—because these things are necessary in order for human beings to survive. Our brains are thought to have evolved a method of rewarding us for behavior that helps us survive: producing dopamine so that we experience pleasure when doing these things and want to do them again.

Dopamine is therefore closely bound up with addiction. Cocaine increases the production of dopamine, and so people have a powerful sense of pleasure when they take the drug. This feeling wears off as the drug is broken down by the body, but the urge to experience the rush of pleasure is powerful, and so drug addicts want to take the drug again and again.

Dopamine is also involved in controlling movement. People with Parkinson's disease produce reduced amounts of dopamine, and this lessens their ability to start and stop movements. It can also cause their hands to shake.

When people take cocaine, the amount of serotonin, noradrenalin, and dopamine at the synapses (nerve junctions) increases dramatically. The result is that the nerves that control the fight-or-flight response, the heart rate and blood pressure, alertness, movement, euphoria, appetite, and body temperature all fire repeatedly. This can be very dangerous for the heart and circulatory system, since it makes them work very hard.

Cocaine not only causes the brain to produce more neurotransmitters, it also disrupts the normal way in which neurotransmitters work in the brain (see the diagram on page 27). Usually, signals or messages travel through the nerves as electrical impulses. When a signal reaches a synapse, a neurotransmitter is released to pass the signal across the junction to the next nerve. Special receptors on the second nerve pick up the neurotransmitter. But then the first nerve sucks back, or recaptures, the neurotransmitter so that it can be used again. The recapturing of the neurotransmitter is important, since it switches off the nerve signal after the message has been sent. Cocaine stops this from happening, and so the nerves keep on sending their messages again and again.

"When I crash after a cocaine hit, it's like I've been thrown out of heaven and I've ended up in hell."
(Elisa)

Taking cocaine results in less neurotransmitter being recaptured. Therefore, after the first effects of the drug have worn off, there is a period when the nerves are not able to work as well as they normally do. The person feels very sleepy, lethargic, cold, depressed, and miserable. This "low" is caused by cocaine, just as much as the initial "high." However, this is not always obvious to cocaine users. They remember the first feelings of energy and euphoria and often, mistakenly, blame the bad feelings on real life. So they want to take more cocaine to feel good again, not realizing that they will also make themselves feel even worse afterward. This cycle can lead to individuals taking more and more cocaine.

Before scientists realized how profoundly cocaine affected people, they performed several experiments with animals to investigate the effects of the drug. They found that the animals that could take as much cocaine as they wanted would continue to take it until they died. The pleasure caused by the drug was so intense that the animals did not stop taking it, even when its toxic effects on their bodies became uncomfortable. This is very unusual behavior. Normally, animals stop taking a drug once it becomes physically unpleasant. The strange behavior of animals taking cocaine is echoed by the

"If there's coke, I can snort it till it's gone. Once you start, you never want it to end."
(Vince)

No stopping

In experiments with rats, scientists have found that the animals normally stop taking a substance once it starts to cause unpleasant symptoms. By contrast, when given cocaine, rats kept on taking the drug, despite its bad effects.

experience of many human cocaine users, who will continue to take the drug until they run out of it or until they overdose.

Overdose

Cocaine works by over-stimulating the nervous system, and it is thought that this effect explains why some cocaine users have convulsions (violent spasms of the body, also known as fits). Convulsions can happen after someone has taken cocaine that is only slightly more concentrated than the dose needed to cause euphoria. It is very easy to overdose on cocaine because the drug is poisonous at quite low concentrations. Convulsions combined with raised body temperature, a racing heartbeat, and high blood pressure can cause cardiac arrest, respiratory failure, and death. Cocaine is even more dangerous when it is mixed with other drugs—especially those that affect heart rate or breathing or those that make people more likely to have convulsions. These include

Symptoms of a cocaine overdose

The first signs of a cocaine overdose are a flushed (red) face and hot, dry skin. These show that the person's body temperature is rising above normal. The person may also have cramps in his or her arms and legs and will feel panicky and anxious. The person may become unconscious or start to have convulsions.

ACTION

- Do not panic, but call an ambulance immediately.
- If the person is conscious, talk to him or her in a calm and reassuring manner. Loosen clothing and try to keep the person cool. Do not allow the person to eat or drink, except for water.
- If the person is having convulsions, make sure that he or she is safe and there is nothing around to bump into. Do not touch the person until the spasms have stopped. Do not put anything in the person's mouth.
- If the person is unconscious, roll him or her into the recovery position. Make sure that the person's airway is not obstructed and stay until the ambulance arrives. Keep a watch on the person's breathing, since you may need to start artificial respiration if the person stops breathing.

heroin, heart-disease medication, and high levels of caffeine or theophylline (a treatment for asthma).

Cocaine and pregnancy

The use of cocaine during pregnancy is very dangerous to the unborn child. Cocaine causes constriction of the blood vessels that supply oxygen and nutrients from the mother to the baby. As a result, the baby may not be able to grow or develop correctly in the mother's womb. The pregnancy may then end in miscarriage or stillbirth. Occasionally, babies of mothers who use cocaine are born dependent on the drug. They suffer distressing withdrawal symptoms

Recovery position
To put people in the recovery position, lie them on their left side, with their right arm and right leg bent. This position lessens the risk of a person choking on his or her vomit.

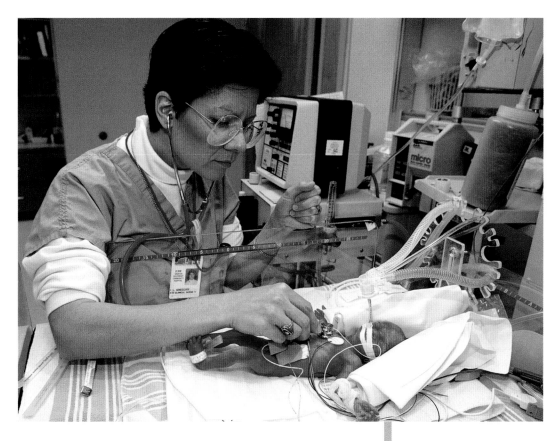

after they are born. Such babies are usually very small and premature (born too early), and this can put them at increased risk of disease and death in the first weeks of life.

The effects of crack and freebase

Freebase and crack are a stronger form of cocaine and are much more potent at lower doses. Smoking crack or freebase can cause extreme elation and feelings of power and limitless strength. These effects are felt within seconds and last between fifteen minutes and one hour. Some users say that crack and freebase cause the most powerful feelings of any street drug. However, the "high" is often quickly followed by equally powerful tiredness, weakness, and feelings of being threatened (sometimes called paranoia). When these profoundly low feelings kick in, users often want to take more of the drug immediately to try to stop the feelings of weakness and anxiety. Of

Born to a crack addict
A premature baby born to a crack addict needs intensive care and may not survive.

course, if they do take more, they feel good for another fifteen minutes or so, but then the bad feeling returns and the high-low cycle continues. Users can often go through many hundreds of dollars worth of a drug in one session, despite the low cost of freebase and crack in comparison to cocaine.

"Crack's taken over my life. I spend all day getting money to buy more, or taking it. I don't know how to stop— part of me doesn't want to, but part of me knows that I have to or I'll die."
(Liam, crack addict)

The long-term consequences of using crack and freebase are the same as for cocaine. In addition, smoking the drugs causes narrowing of the blood vessels in the lungs. This can result in ulceration of the lung tissue and cause bleeding.

Heavy use of crack and freebase often leaves users with profound psychological problems. Many develop a deep sense of paranoia and are suspicious of everyone. They can also be very aggressive, particularly to anyone who tries to stop them from taking the drug. They may become violent and have delusions (believe things that are imaginary). For some long-term crack users, these effects can be permanent.

The extreme high produced by crack and freebase makes them very addictive drugs, even more so than cocaine itself. In the next chapter, we investigate the biological mechanisms and other factors that affect addiction. We also investigate withdrawal from cocaine and how people can recover from cocaine addiction.

"My brother got in with a gang that did crack. It destroyed him and us. He turned into a monster, lying, stealing. He started hitting us—he attacked Mom with a bread knife when she tried to stop him from going out to get drugs. Crack is evil."
(Shelley)

3 Cocaine Addiction
How It Develops

Medical experts say that someone is addicted to a drug if he or she uses it repetitively and compulsively, despite the negative consequences this has. Substances to which people become addicted activate the basic "reward system" in the brain, which responds to normal pleasures such as food, sex, and love. The system is made up of nerve cells (neurons), and it can be stimulated by an electrical current. Scientific experiments have shown that animals and humans will do an incredible variety of things in order to set off an electric current that stimulates the reward system; in other words, they will do an incredible variety of things to have the experience of pleasure. These experiments have helped doctors to understand how addiction works.

The neurotransmitter (brain chemical) dopamine is closely connected with the experience of pleasure. Drugs that are addictive usually directly affect the production of dopamine. As we saw earlier, cocaine causes large amounts of dopamine to be released into the junctions between nerves. This makes cocaine highly addictive.

The importance of pleasure

Pleasure is very important in our lives. If you think about the activities that give us pleasure naturally, you will see that they usually

Pleasure centers

In 1954 scientists James Olds and Peter Milner discovered that rats could learn how to press a lever in order to set off an electric current that would stimulate the pleasure centers in their brains. Other experiments found that, if rats were forced to choose between food and electrical stimulation of their pleasure centers, they would choose to do without food and starve themselves in order to keep stimulating their pleasure centers.

have some function in helping us survive. We get pleasure from eating a nice meal. When we are very hungry, we get pleasure from eating nearly anything. If we are thirsty, we experience pleasure when we drink. Love and sex are sources of pleasure,

Satisfying hunger
Eating is pleasurable and also necessary for our survival.

What makes a drug addictive?

In order for a drug to be considered addictive, it has to cause one or more of the following things to happen:

- The drug has to affect users in such a way that they continue to use it regularly and repetitively, despite any unpleasant effects it may have on their bodies or their lives.
- Users have to experience a physical need or a psychological need to use the drug, and the need has to be so strong that they feel compelled to keep using the drug.
- The drug has to activate the parts of the brain that are activated by normal pleasures, such as food, sex, or laughing.
- Usually, the drug has to cause unpleasant symptoms for users when they stop using it.

as are laughing with friends, spending time with loving relatives, and exercise. All these things are necessary for our health and social well-being. If we did not do these things, our survival as individuals and as a social group would be threatened. Imagine how difficult life would be if there was no love and friendship in the world.

Pleasure is a motivator (sometimes called a reinforcer). This means that the pleasure you experience when you do something makes you more likely (motivates you) to do it again. This "pleasure system" helps you to survive. Animals and humans who have damage to their pleasure system behave very differently from people whose system is working. They are still able to eat, drink, work, and reproduce, but they simply do not want to. There is little or no pleasure in these activities, and so they do not bother doing them. They lose motivation to take part in living.

Cocaine causes a huge rush of pleasure. But, because it has used all the dopamine reserves in your brain (see page 29), it also causes the absence of pleasure. Cocaine users therefore have some experience of a world without

Togetherness
The pleasure people get from loving family relationships motivates them to care for each other and keep the family together.

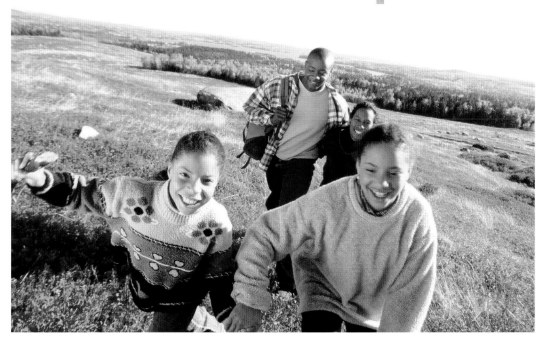

pleasure, and it is an unpleasant place. They feel very low and miserable, sad, tired, and irritable, and these feelings are made worse by the memory of the pleasure they did experience. Pleasure is such a powerful motivator that cocaine users feel desperate to experience the feeling again. They do not remember that the drug caused the misery as well as the euphoria. So they take more of the drug, desperately trying to recapture the first rush of pleasure. This is the beginning of addiction. Some cocaine users will continue taking cocaine until they overdose or they run out.

The development of addiction

Addiction usually develops slowly. People do not get addicted to cocaine the first time they try it. The changes happen gradually, as the brain gets used to the drug and adapts to it. The chemicals in the brain exist in a finely tuned balance and the brain has complicated systems to make sure that the balance is not disturbed. If someone takes a drug such as cocaine, which causes large amounts of dopamine to be released, the brain tries to minimize the disruption caused by the drug. It may reduce the amount of dopamine available to be released. Less dopamine available makes drug users less able to experience pleasure from normal activities and less able to experience pleasure from taking the drug the next time they try it. They may then take more of the drug, or use it more often, to try to experience the same feelings of pleasure they achieved the first time.

"I'm not ready to give up coke yet. I need it too much. Without cocaine the world seems empty to me."
(Alice, cocaine addict)

A yearning or longing for a drug is called a craving, and various things can trigger a craving for cocaine. Memory is very important. For example, seeing equipment that has been used before to take the drug can be enough to start a craving. This may be injecting equipment, or paper money, which is often rolled into a tube through which to snort cocaine, or any items involved in the user's ritual of cocaine use. Seeing people associated with the drug, or visiting places where the user has taken the drug, or experiencing certain sights, smells, sounds, and tastes are all capable of triggering a craving for cocaine.

Eventually the drug takes over the experience of pleasure completely so that, when there is no drug, the brain's "reward system" does not work correctly. Cocaine addicts no longer get pleasure from food, warmth, or love—but only from cocaine. The inability to feel pleasure is a powerful reason for continuing to take a drug. For a few addicts, these changes may be permanent. However, the pleasure system of most cocaine addicts will recover eventually, once they stop taking the drug.

"I've lost my family and friends. All I have now is crack. I have to face up to it, or it will ruin the rest of my life, too." (Darren, crack addict)

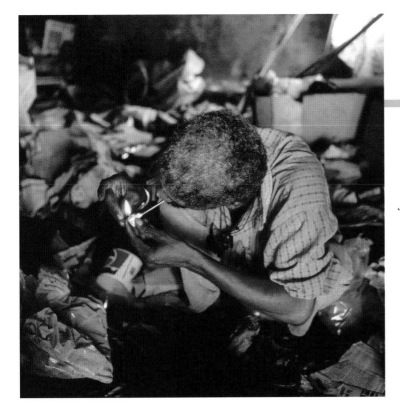

Smoking crack
For crack addicts, the drug is more important than their living environment, their family, or their friends. This addict was photographed on the streets of Panama City, Panama.

What causes addiction?

So why do some people get addicted and others do not? Recent research seems to suggest that there may be a part of our genetic makeup that can make us more likely to become addicted. Studies of alcoholics and their children have shown some differences between them and non-alcoholic families. It is thought that some people may inherit a predisposition to become addicted to alcohol and other substances. Animal studies seem to support this idea, but the responsible genes have not yet been fully mapped out. However, having a genetic vulnerability to addiction does not mean that the person will inevitably go on to become an addict. Similarly, not having the gene does not necessarily mean that someone will not become an addict. Environment, behavior, circumstance, and free will all have a part to play.

Self-medication

A large number of cocaine addicts also have psychiatric conditions, such as attention deficit hyperactivity disorder (ADHD), anxiety disorders, mood disorders, and personality disorders. One idea is that some people may take cocaine in an attempt to treat themselves for these types of problems. This is called "self-medication" and may be another cause of addiction.

The term "addictive personality" is often talked about in magazines, though it is not clear exactly what this personality is. There is some evidence that people who tend to act in particular ways may be more likely than others to develop an addiction. People who are risk-takers and impulsive are more likely to try a drug in the first place, and people who have a tendency to be obsessive (thinking about one particular thing to the exclusion of everything else) find it harder to break addiction.

Environmental factors, such as where you live and who you live or work with, also affect your risk of becoming addicted to drugs. You are more likely to become an addict if you grew up in a household with a substance-abusing parent, if your friends abuse drugs, or if you have been abused as a child. Experimenting with tobacco, marijuana, and alcohol at a young age also increases your chances of addiction. Women, in particular, are more likely to abuse drugs when they are older if they suffered abuse as a child. None of this means that you are bound to become an addict if you have experienced problems such as these, or if you have a risk-taking or obsessive personality. You always have free choice in what you do with your body and whether or not you take drugs.

Not the type

"I didn't think I'd get addicted to cocaine. I'm not the type. My family wasn't poor and I had a happy childhood. Some guys at college kept talking about how wonderful cocaine was. They said it was okay. They teased me about being scared, so I tried it. It was great—nothing bad happened. I just stayed awake a long time. So I thought this is okay and I started taking it—Saturday night, parties, that sort of thing, just on weekends. Then Monday mornings became harder to handle. Exams were starting, money was running short, and I needed some extra help to get through. So I used cocaine to keep me going through the week. It just gradually increased. I felt so bad when I hadn't taken it. All I could think of was getting enough money together to get the next 'line.' I started dealing a little, just to friends, and things gradually got out of control. It was like living in a dream. I looked in the mirror one morning and didn't recognize myself. I was not the man I had thought I was going to be. I had no job. I had argued so much with my family that they avoided me and, instead of being someone with a future, I was a small-time drug dealer with a habit to support. So I made a decision then and there. It had to stop. Get control of my life again or end up in prison or dead. I went to my doctor and got myself into a detox program. It has not been easy, but I'm not going to let it beat me."

(Mark, age 25, recovering cocaine addict)

Peer pressure

Being part of a group that takes drugs has a big impact on the likelihood of your becoming addicted. This is partly because some people in the group can probably get hold of drugs for you and partly because of peer pressure. With people who use cocaine and call themselves friends, it is very hard to resist the pressure to try the drug. Other members of the group may pressure you into joining them. They might say that trying the drug is a test of loyalty to the group, or tease you that you are too scared to try it.

How you react to this pressure can change the course of your life. The pressure to do what your friends want you to do can be enormous. However, you have to decide whether this is the way you want your life to go and whether you are willing to risk your life just to conform with people that want you to take that risk. Having a clear idea of the risks involved in taking cocaine and thinking about how you would deal with this sort of situation before it happens can help you to stay safe and achieve the outcome you want.

Environmental factors can also help people resist addiction. If you have a loving, supportive family and friends, a stable and secure life, no family history of substance abuse, and a good education, you are far less likely to become an addict. However, it must be remembered that cocaine, and especially crack cocaine, are extremely addictive drugs, and whenever cocaine, crack, or freebase use has become fashionable, many people from stable, loving families with no history of substance abuse have become addicts. Anyone can become addicted to cocaine, no matter who they are or where they live. The next chapter considers how addicts can find help when they give up cocaine.

"I've been offered crack and cocaine but I've never taken them. I'm not that stupid."
(Sally, student)

4 Recovering from Addiction
Withdrawal and Treatment

Withdrawal

When drug users stop taking a drug they have become used to taking, the process is known as withdrawal. Withdrawal from cocaine use is an unpleasant experience, but it is not usually dangerous or life-threatening, unlike withdrawal from alcohol or heroin. People who have only used cocaine a few times and for limited periods may have very few symptoms of withdrawal.

Cocaine works by over-stimulating the brain and body, and the brain seeks to restore balance by reducing the stimulation. Therefore, when people stop using cocaine, they become exhausted, low, and depressed. People who stop taking cocaine often become very hungry, too. This is because cocaine tends to decrease the appetite, and so the person may not have eaten well for a long time.

Withdrawal symptoms

The symptoms of withdrawal from cocaine include:
- *Agitation*
- *Sadness*
- *Craving for cocaine*
- *Inability to experience pleasure*
- *Hunger*
- *Insomnia with an intense need for sleep*
- *Oversleeping*
- *Tiredness*
- *Anxiety*
- *Lack of energy*

Brain scans
The first of these brain scans shows a slice, front (top) to back, of a normal human brain. The second shows a brain four months after withdrawal from heavy cocaine use. The areas colored yellow are areas of high activity. The lack of these areas in ex–cocaine users' brains are the reason for their loss of energy and pleasure.

The biggest problem for people withdrawing from cocaine is the absence of pleasure in their lives. When heavy users of cocaine stop taking the drug, their brains respond by decreasing the amount of dopamine available, and so they are unable to experience pleasure for awhile. How long the absence of pleasure lasts depends on several factors, including the length of time over which users have taken cocaine and how much they took. It also depends on the individual. Some people may be unable to feel pleasure for weeks or months following giving up cocaine.

Taking the first step

Admitting that you are addicted to cocaine is the first step on the road to recovery. Drug counselors use a series of questions and answers such as the ones listed below to help people who take cocaine, crack, and freebase think seriously about how the drug is affecting their lives. Answering "yes" to any of the questions below is a warning sign that you may have an addiction problem.

- *Do you ever feel you would do anything to get some cocaine/crack/freebase?*
- *Do you ever feel guilty about using cocaine/crack/freebase?*
- *Do you ever use cocaine/crack/freebase to help you operate or function normally?*
- *Have you ever missed school or work or not fulfilled your responsibilities because you had taken or needed to get cocaine/crack/freebase?*
- *Have you ever stolen anything in order to obtain cocaine/crack/freebase?*
- *Has anyone ever confronted you about using drugs?*

The inability to experience pleasure is a major factor that makes cocaine users go back to using the drug, even though they intended to stop taking it. Life without pleasure is a very bleak place, and the desire to feel pleasure again can be hard to resist. It can cause an intense and sometimes overwhelming craving for the drug. Cravings like this can suddenly occur again many months or even years following withdrawal from heavy cocaine use.

The symptoms that people experience when they stop using cocaine can vary. This is because about 76 percent of cocaine addicts have at least one psychiatric condition in addition to their addiction to cocaine. These conditions include mood disorders, anxiety disorders, personality disorders, and attention deficit hyperactivity disorder (ADHD). They can make the feelings associated with withdrawal from cocaine much worse and may result in severe depression and the risk of suicide.

Suicide
The depression suffered by some cocaine addicts leads them to attempt suicide. This is a particular risk for addicts who also use depressant drugs such as alcohol or heroin.

Cocaine addicts are also often addicted to other drugs as well—often alcohol, opiates, or amphetamines. This can make withdrawal from cocaine much more dangerous because of the effects of the other drugs. Alcohol and heroin are both depressant drugs, which can cause the depression following cocaine withdrawal to be unpredictably severe. The person therefore has an increased risk of suicide or self-harm. Because of this, a doctor should supervise people who have a long-established addiction to cocaine during withdrawal from the drug.

Group support
Many people recovering from addiction to drugs find group counseling a helpful part of their treatment.

Treatment

Drug addiction is treatable, and the majority of addicts are able to achieve a complete recovery. Treatment for cocaine addiction needs to be appropriate for each different individual. There are no specific medical treatments to help people withdraw from cocaine, and most doctors do not prescribe any medication for this period. However, some organizations specializing in narcotic withdrawal have found that it can be very effective for addicts to take vitamin and mineral supplements at the same time they work through a program designed to help them learn to manage in the world without drugs. In general, it seems that the more help addicts are given, the greater the likelihood that they will remain drug-free in the long term.

Because so many people addicted to cocaine have an underlying psychiatric condition, such as attention deficit hyperactivity disorder, withdrawal is much more successful if they have appropriate medication to treat this problem.

"My counselor made all the difference. Having someone there who really understands how difficult the cravings are has given me the strength to struggle on."
(Amy-Louise, recovering crack addict)

The ultimate goal of treatment for cocaine addiction is to help people to stop using the drug and to return to a normal mental state. Treatment usually involves helping users move away from their normal drug-taking environment and helping them to withdraw safely under medical supervision.

Non-residential support

Non-residential support for recovering cocaine addicts is most suitable for people who already have good support from family and friends and have not been dependent on cocaine for very long. Because of the highly addictive nature of crack cocaine and freebase, addicts to these drugs tend to find it even more difficult to recover from addiction and need lots of support. Recovering addicts can be helped by group counseling, family counseling, and behavior therapy. Behavior therapy involves learning other ways to behave in situations, different ways to cope with relationships, and ways of coping with the difficulties of life without resorting to drugs.

"I became a counselor for people giving up cocaine after I had gone through the program myself. I wanted to reach out and help others to beat this terrible illness."
(Alvin, addiction counselor)

Self-help groups, such as Narcotics Anonymous or Cocaine Anonymous, provide a program that includes group counseling and individual support. These types of programs can be particularly successful, since the support comes from other recovering addicts who can understand the problems involved in overcoming addiction.

Short-term treatment programs

Short-term treatment programs usually last between three and six weeks. Cocaine addicts are supervised during withdrawal, at a residential unit, and afterward they receive support for the first few months of abstinence from cocaine use. This type of treatment can include exercise programs and nutritional therapy to help individuals regain their health and strength. It also often includes individual, group, and family therapy and education about drugs, addiction, and life skills, in order to maximize a recovering addict's chances of staying drug-free.

"I went to a clinic for the first stage of detox. Being away from the possibility of scoring [buying drugs] meant that I could get through that first stage." (Ethan, age 24, recovering cocaine addict)

Therapeutic communities

Therapeutic communities, where people stay for between six and twelve months, can be very successful at helping cocaine addicts overcome addiction. Residential help of this length is more common in the United States than in Europe, which favors shorter programs. The communities tend to be more suitable for people with a history of long-term, heavy cocaine abuse and who have serious difficulty overcoming the psychological problems caused by cocaine, crack, and freebase. The treatment focuses on helping individuals learn how to live in a crime-free, drug-free environment.

Psychological therapy

Psychological therapies include behavior therapy, in which the aim is to change an individual's behavior, and cognitive therapy, which aims to help people manage the way they think and behave. The ultimate goal of these therapies is to help cocaine addicts regain control over their lives. They often have to relearn how to find pleasure in the natural things of life, such as friends and family.

A new life

Recovering addicts need to remove themselves from the places where they were in contact with the drug. They will need additional support to cope in new surroundings.

Often, cocaine addicts, and particularly those addicted to crack or freebase, need to change their lifestyles completely in order to avoid being back in a situation where they could restart taking the drug. Changing their lifestyles involves making new friends and even moving to a different area. The recovering addicts need support in the development of new relationships. They are also encouraged to join counseling or support groups in which they learn strategies to resist temptation and find support to help them stay drug-free.

Ongoing support

Treating addiction is a long process. Cravings for the drug can last for many months, sometimes for the rest of the person's life. Self-help groups, such as Cocaine Anonymous and Narcotics Anonymous, offer ongoing support for recovering cocaine addicts. This can be vital in helping them resist the temptation to start taking the drug again.

5 Cocaine in Today's World
Its Impact on Society

Although the number of people who use cocaine is relatively small, cocaine use has a profound impact on our society. Dealing in cocaine, crack, and freebase is associated with crime, violence, and prostitution. Crimes are committed by people who produce and smuggle drugs and by addicts who need to get money to buy the drug. Also, crimes of violence are sometimes committed by people coming down from a crack hit who are experiencing paranoia.

The trade in cocaine affects the health and welfare of thousands of people around the world, not only those who use the drug. This includes people who are coerced or tricked into smuggling cocaine across borders. Having a family member who is addicted to cocaine can be extremely stressful, and stress can badly affect a person's health, making them more vulnerable to illness. It can also be very stressful living in an area where crack or freebase dealers operate.

Crime scene
Money, a revolver, and bags of crack cocaine, seized when police raided a crack house, are signs of the life of crime led by drug dealers.

International cocaine laws

In the United States, cocaine is classified as a Schedule 1 controlled drug. This means that it is illegal to possess or supply the drug to others. It is also illegal to import or export cocaine, crack, or freebase, and to allow your premises to be used for the production or supply of the drugs. Penalties vary from state to state.

In the United Kingdom, cocaine, crack, and freebase are Class A Schedule 2 drugs. It is illegal to buy or possess the drugs without a prescription. It is also illegal to supply the drugs to others, to import, export, or process them, or to allow your premises to be used for production, supply, or taking of the drug. Addiction to cocaine is a notifiable disease in Britain, which means that doctors who have reason to believe that a patient is addicted to cocaine, crack, or freebase are obliged to report it to the police.

All members of the European Union classify illegal drugs in accordance with United Nations Conventions. It is therefore illegal to supply, possess, import, export, or process cocaine, crack, and freebase across the entire EU.

Producers, cartels, and mules

Most of the cocaine available around the world is grown and processed in one of three countries: Peru, Bolivia, and Colombia. However, it is in Colombia that the majority of cocaine is processed. Cocaine production is controlled by a few very rich and powerful gangs, called cartels. Over recent years, cartels from Brazil and Mexico have become more powerful.

Drug cartels are responsible for an enormous amount of misery, not just for the drug addicts they supply with drugs, but throughout the whole supply chain. One group of people who are particularly vulnerable are the "mules."

These are often poor and desperate people who are recruited or forced to smuggle cocaine through customs into the United States and Europe.

Originally, most cocaine was smuggled across the border into the United States from Mexico, or flown in using light aircraft from the Caribbean, particularly Puerto Rico and Haiti. In the late 1980s, the U.S. Drug Enforcement Agency began to warn that the cocaine market would soon be saturated—in other words, there would be more cocaine available than drug users to buy it. They foresaw that drug cartels would begin to increase the amount of cocaine they smuggled into Europe and Australia. This proved to be the case, and in the 1990s the amounts of cocaine seized by police and customs officials in the United Kingdom increased enormously.

The constant search

Customs officers around the world are constantly searching for hidden drug caches. Search dogs are often used, with a high success rate.

Cocaine smugglers use a variety of routes to get the cocaine into a target country. Some cocaine arrives in Europe through Spain and Portugal, and a large amount arrives in the United Kingdom from Jamaica. A report from the United Nations in February 2003 claimed that one in ten of all passengers on flights from Jamaica was smuggling drugs into the United Kingdom. Some people feel that this figure underestimates the amount of drug smuggling on these flights. Women caught smuggling drugs into Great Britain make up more than half of the population in some British women's prisons. Drug cartel bosses are rumored to pay people $2,600 per trip for trafficking drugs.

Poor women are targeted as mules. A method used to conceal the cocaine they are carrying is for them to swallow packages of more than 1 lb (0.5 kg) of the drug, wrapped in the fingers of latex gloves or in condoms. There is a high risk of these packages bursting, and, if they do, the carrier receives an enormous dose of cocaine and dies. Nonetheless, many women risk death in this way because they feel that smuggling the drugs is the only way

Coming through customs

"We get lots of smugglers arriving through the airport. Many of the cocaine smugglers come in from Jamaica or other Caribbean countries. Others come in from Spain and Portugal. It's a tragedy. Some of them are so frightened. They look nervous as they come through, especially if they've swallowed packets of cocaine. They are risking their lives. Some of them even come through with their children. They're called mules by drug gangs. The gangs don't care about the risks these people take. They treat them worse than animals. I feel especially sorry for the women. Some of them are forced to smuggle the drugs. Others are so poor that they think it's worth the risk for the money. Lots of them end up in prison here. Some people are tricked into smuggling drugs. It's slipped into their luggage. Others have drugs sewn into their clothes. It's amazing where they put it."
(Andrew, customs official)

for them to get the money that they desperately need for their families. Consequently, there are many children in both Jamaica and the United Kingdom whose mothers are in jail for smuggling offenses. Families are split up, and the suffering increases.

"These men said if I did this one trip I would be rich—able to send my daughter to college. But now I'm stuck here in prison. Ten years . . . I won't be able to see my little girl grow up."
(Hester)

Street crime

Since the 1980s, the price of cocaine has gone down and availability has increased, especially of crack and freebase. This has resulted in an increase in cocaine use in some areas of the world, particularly in Europe. In some areas of the United Kingdom, in particular, crack cocaine is thought to be growing in popularity, and addiction to crack is involved in a wide range of street crimes, including prostitution, mugging, car crime, and burglary. However, this effect is very localized. Some inner-city areas suffer from an explosion in crack-related crime, whereas the drug is hardly heard of in other areas.

Drugs have a big impact on our society via crime. The British Home Office Department of Research Development and Statistics researched five areas of the United Kingdom in 1998 and found that, of all those arrested, 61 percent had taken at least one illegal drug, 46 percent tested positive for marijuana, 18 percent had taken opiates, and 10 percent had taken cocaine. Nearly 50 percent said that drug use was connected with the crime for which they were arrested. The cost of one drug addict to society, in property crime, theft, and prostitution, can be more than $600,000 per year.

The spread of crack cocaine use in the United Kingdom, the United States, and Europe is thought to be related to the activities of Jamaican and other Caribbean gangs. The same groups are thought to be involved in orchestrating the smuggling of cocaine. Fighting between rival gangs in inner-city areas is the cause of much misery and fear and, sometimes, death.

A crack house

"This used to be a good neighborhood—people weren't angels, but you could sleep at night. Now there's crashing and banging all night. I was woken up at 3 A.M. last night by people swearing and screaming. It was frightening. The police came and everything. Mom said that someone had been hurt—a fight, I think. The man across the street has had to move out, but he can't sell his house. It all went wrong after the people across the street moved in. Lots of people are always coming and going. My friend Sam says they are selling drugs—he says it's a crack house. Lots of cars have been broken into, and people have had stuff stolen. I'm really scared they'll come in here one day. The people who live next to them are scared to go out and scared to stay in. It's really horrible. The police know about it—they get reported enough. I just don't know what is going to happen."
(Darcy, age 14)

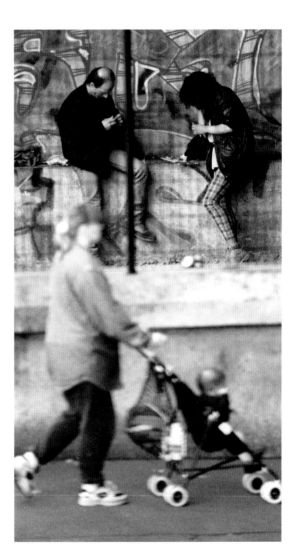

Gang war

Crack cocaine use is associated with inner-city areas and "street gangs" made up mainly of teen males. Crack is made and sold by some gangs to make money to fund their own drug habits. Crack often makes people feel very anxious and violent. Many people think that the violence and crime associated with street gangs are fueled by crack.

The individual cost

Cocaine addiction has a huge effect on individual addicts and their families. Regular use of cocaine, crack, and freebase is expensive. Funding an addiction can become the focus of an addict's attention. Everything else is of less importance than the next fix. This can lead to debts building up, stealing from other members of the family, lying, and using funds intended for other purposes for drugs and crime.

People who are dependent on cocaine, crack, or freebase also often behave in a violent and unpredictable way, which can further isolate them from their families and loved ones. Family and relationships are not as important to the cocaine addict as the next "hit." The drug replaces the need for affection, and the addict will not let anything get in the way of the next dose. The distortion of reality caused by the drug prevents addicts from seeing the

Family life

"My brother doesn't live with us anymore. He got addicted to crack. It all started when he was sixteen and he got into what Dad called a 'rebellious phase.' He became angry, as if he were a different person. He wanted to hurt all of us, even me. I think something must have happened, but he never mentioned anything. He got in with a group of friends—though I wouldn't call them friends. They hung out together and took drugs. Somehow they got my brother to take them, too. I didn't think he would do things like that. I thought I knew my brother. I thought he was smarter than that. They started taking crack. He would come home late and was angry and frightened. We had to be so careful. Anything I said, he would take the wrong way. It was scary. He started stealing from home to buy drugs. He even stole from me. Mom and Dad had to hide their money and credit cards. He sold the TV one day—we thought we had been robbed, but it turned out that it was him. He sold it to buy more crack. Mom and Dad were so upset. They keep asking what they did wrong, how they can change it. I don't think anything can change it. He ran away from home after that. I feel so angry with him. I hate him, but I wish he would come home."
(Foley, age 13)

damage they are doing to the people around them. They often do not recognize that there is anything wrong. Cocaine and crack users have a greater tendency to become aggressive and violent than people who do not take these drugs. This aggression and violence can be especially difficult to live with and are responsible for many relationship breakdowns.

"Crack became like air to me. I couldn't live without it. I had to have it, no matter what. I can't stand to think about some of the things I did to get it. I feel so ashamed."
(Candy, recovering crack addict)

Crack users tend to band together in areas called crack houses. The amount of crime and violence that centers around these areas can destroy communities. In some parts of the country, residents have banded together to try to drive crack dealers and users away from their neighborhood.

Keeping the problem in perspective

This chapter has looked at the problems that cocaine use causes in society. However, the level of cocaine use needs to be kept in perspective. The

Community spirit

When people band together, they have the power to make their neighborhood a safe and pleasant place to live.

most abused drug in the world is alcohol, which is a legal drug. Despite the lower price and increased availability of cocaine, crack, and freebase today, the vast majority of people will never take these drugs. Cocaine is not a part of normal life, and of the people who do try it, the vast majority will not continue using it or progress to addiction.

Staying in control

Being well-informed is one of the best defenses against addiction. If you know the facts about cocaine and crack, and their potential for harm and addiction, you are less likely to be fooled by someone trying to tell you that the drugs are harmless. It is a good idea to think about situations you might find yourself in before they happen. If you were at a party and someone offered you a crack-laced cigarette, or a line of cocaine, what would you do? If you want to try it, are you fully aware of the risks you

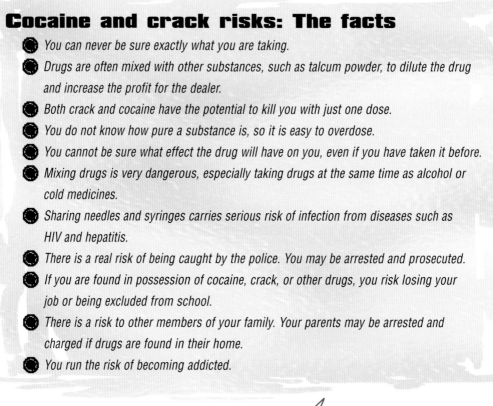

Cocaine and crack risks: The facts

- You can never be sure exactly what you are taking.
- Drugs are often mixed with other substances, such as talcum powder, to dilute the drug and increase the profit for the dealer.
- Both crack and cocaine have the potential to kill you with just one dose.
- You do not know how pure a substance is, so it is easy to overdose.
- You cannot be sure what effect the drug will have on you, even if you have taken it before.
- Mixing drugs is very dangerous, especially taking drugs at the same time as alcohol or cold medicines.
- Sharing needles and syringes carries serious risk of infection from diseases such as HIV and hepatitis.
- There is a real risk of being caught by the police. You may be arrested and prosecuted.
- If you are found in possession of cocaine, crack, or other drugs, you risk losing your job or being excluded from school.
- There is a risk to other members of your family. Your parents may be arrested and charged if drugs are found in their home.
- You run the risk of becoming addicted.

are taking? Do you know what it is you are being offered? If you do not want to take it, how will you say "no"? Practicing what to do in different situations is called role-play. Role-playing with friends is helpful, since you can discuss different ways of handling a situation. It is impossible to say exactly what to do in each situation, because your life, experience, and environment are different from anyone else's.

If someone approaches you to sell cocaine or other drugs, or you are worried that a friend has taken drugs, then you need to tell someone. It is usually best to tell your parents, but if you feel unable to talk to them, then a teacher or school counselor may be able to help. In some places there are groups of drug counselors your own age to whom you can go for advice or support. Whatever you do, do not worry in silence.

Role play

Role-playing different situations in which you may be offered drugs prepares you to deal confidently with real-life events.

Glossary

addiction   condition in which people need a drug to relieve unpleasant symptoms experienced when they stop taking it. This happens because the body has adapted to the drug being present, so when it is not present the body craves it.

addictive   having the potential to cause addiction

anesthetic   drug that reduces the ability of the body to experience pain

atherosclerosis   fat that coats the inside of blood vessels and makes them narrower

circulatory system   system involved in moving blood around the body. It includes the heart, veins, arteries, and capillaries.

coma   unconsciousness

compulsively   following a strong, irrational urge to act in a particular way

convulsion   involuntary, violent spasm of the muscles of the body

craving   desperate and urgent longing

dependent   people are said to be dependent on a drug when they have a compelling desire, physical or psychological, to keep taking it

depressant drugs   drugs that depress the nervous system, rather than exciting it

depression   treatable medical condition in which the individual feels hopeless, inadequate, and unhappy. It is usually accompanied by sleep problems and appetite changes.

derivative   something that is produced from something else

detox   detoxification, the act of ridding the body of toxins or poisons

dopamine   neurotransmitter that is involved in purposeful movement, hormone release, euphoria, and the way we experience pleasure

drug   chemical that is taken into people's bodies in order to change their physical or mental state

euphoria   feeling of extreme well-being and elation

genetic   carried or passed on through the genes. Genes are parts of your body cells containing characteristics that are inherited from your biological parents and ancestors.

hallucination   perception of something that is not really there. This can involve seeing, hearing, smelling, tasting, or feeling.

heart attack   when the heart suddenly stops working correctly. Heart attacks are a medical emergency and can result in death.

hepatitis   highly infectious virus passed on by contact with body fluids such as blood or sperm. It causes serious inflammation of the liver and can be fatal.

high   slang for the experience of being under the influence of a psychoactive drug

HIV   Human Immunodeficiency Virus, a virus that attacks part of the body's immune system. It is passed on by contact with infected blood, sperm, or saliva.

hormone	one of a group of chemicals produced by the body that affect the way the body functions
infertility	biological inability to have children
miscarriage	premature ending of a pregnancy, when the fetus dies
mucous membrane	body tissue that produces mucus in order to lubricate an area and protect it from infection. The lungs are one organ of the body that has a mucous membrane.
narcotics	drugs that affect the central nervous system, producing dizziness, euphoria, and ultimately unconsciousness and death
neuro-transmitters	chemicals that transmit a message across a junction (synapse) between two nerves. They are mainly found in the brain and spinal cord.
noradrenalin	neurotransmitter that regulates the body's physical and mental reaction to stress
opiates	drugs produced from the sap of the opium poppy, such as codeine, morphine, and heroin
overdose	taking too much of a drug. This usually causes physical or mental damage.
paranoia	mental condition in which a person thinks that everyone is out to get him or her. It includes intense, irrational fear and suspicion.
Parkinson's disease	disease that causes a lack of dopamine. This results in tremor, masklike facial expression, loss of coordination, fatigue, and depression.

psychedelic movement	1960s movement in which people became interested in the mind-altering properties of drugs and wanted to explore the creative potential of their drug-induced experiences in art, music, and philosophy
psychiatrist	person medically qualified to treat diseases of the mind
psychoactive	affecting the brain and behavior
psychosis	serious mental condition usually involving illusions, confusion, delusions, and hallucinations, with the sufferer not realizing that he or she is ill
ritual	ceremony or sequence of actions performed the same way every time, to make the event seem special
serotonin	neurotransmitter that regulates the body clock, appetite, sleep patterns, and body temperature
smoking	breathing in the chemicals produced by burning drugs
snorting	sniffing a substance into the nose
stimulant	drug that "stimulates" (increases the activity level of) the body and mind
stroke	sudden event that causes the rupture of blood vessels in the brain
sympathetic nervous system	division of the central nervous system that controls many involuntary actions of the organs, glands, and other parts of the body
vaso-constriction	narrowing of blood vessels caused by tightening of small muscles in the blood vessel walls

Resources

Further Reading

Carroll, Marilyn. *Cocaine and Crack.* Berkeley Heights, N.J.: Enslow, 2001.

Connolly, Sean. *Cocaine.* Chicago: Heinemann, 2001.

Robbins, Paul R. *Crack and Cocaine Drug Dangers.* Berkeley Heights, N.J.: Enslow, 2001.

Organizations

Center for Substance Abuse Prevention
5600 Fishers Lane, Rockwall II
Rockville, MD 20857
(310) 443-0365
www.samhsa.gov

Child Welfare League of America
440 First Street NW
Washington, DC 20001
(202) 638-2952
www.cwla.org

Cocaine Anonymous
3740 Overland Ave., Suite C
Los Angeles, CA 90034
www.ca.org

DARE America
(drug abuse resistance and education)
P.O. Box 775
Dumfries, VA 22026
(703) 860-3273
www.dare.com

Disclaimer
The website addresses (URLs) included in this book were valid at the time of going to press. However, because of the nature of the Internet, it is possible that some addresses may have changed, or sites may have changed or closed down since publication. While the author and the publishers regret any inconvenience this may cause readers, no responsibility for any such changes can be accepted by either the author or the publishers.

Index